FISH FARMING FOR

BEGINNER

Essential Techniques, Equipment, And Strategies For Successful Aquaculture, Sustainable Practices, And Maximizing Profits

Holden bodhio

Contents

DISCLAIMER

The information provided in this book, is intended for educational and informational purposes only. The content is based on research, personal experiences, and general knowledge about farming. It is not intended to substitute professional advice or expert consultation. Readers are encouraged to seek professional guidance when implementing any practices or techniques discussed in this book.

The author and publisher make no representations or warranties of any kind regarding the accuracy, applicability, or completeness of the contents of this book. Any reliance you place on such information is strictly at your own risk. The author and publisher shall not be held liable for any damages, losses, or injuries resulting from the use of the information provided.

Additionally, the author does not endorse, recommend, or affiliate with any individual, product, service, website, organization, or brand mentioned or referenced in this book. Any such references are solely for informational purposes, and no warranty or guarantee is implied. The inclusion of these references does not imply any endorsement or partnership by the author.

By reading this book, you acknowledge and accept that the author and publisher are not responsible for any consequences arising from your use of the information provided.

CHAPTER ONE

Overview Of Fish Farming

Fish are cultivated in controlled surroundings in a method called aquaculture, or fish farming. Due to the decline of wild fish supplies and the rising demand for fish as a source of protein worldwide, this business has seen substantial growth in recent years. Fish farming provides a regulated technique of producing high-quality fish, making it a sustainable alternative to satisfy this need. This chapter offers a thorough overview of fish farming, examining its history, importance, and various fish cultivation techniques.

An Overview Of Fish Farming

Fish farming has been around for ages, having its roots in the ancient societies of Egypt and China. To maximize productivity and sustainability, contemporary fish farming has, nonetheless, greatly changed by embracing cutting-edge technology and scientific approaches. Raising fish in tanks, ponds, or other enclosures allows for careful monitoring and management of their development and well-being.

Although raising fish for sustenance is the main objective of fish farming, it also helps to replace wild populations, generate aquarium-attractive fish, and provide revenue for small-scale farmers. Depending on the species being raised, freshwater or saltwater conditions may be used for fish farming.

Over the last two decades, the business has grown quickly and become an essential part of the world food system. Nearly half of the world's fish supply currently comes from aquaculture, according to the Food and Agriculture Organisation (FAO), making it an essential component of food security and nutrition.

The Value And Advantages Of Fish Farming

Fish, a very healthy and sought-after source of protein, is in great demand, and fish farming is essential to supply this need. The demand for sustainable food production technologies has never been greater, with projections indicating that the world's population will approach 10 billion by the year 2050. Both large- and small-scale farmers find fish farming to be an appealing alternative due to its many important advantages.

1. Sustainable Food Production: Fish farming enables the controlled and sustainable production of fish, in contrast to conventional fishing techniques that depend on wild fish populations. Without diminishing natural resources, fish farmers may provide a steady supply of fish by carefully controlling the breeding, feeding, and harvesting procedures.

2. Economic Growth and Job Creation: Millions of people worldwide get their income and job prospects from fish farming, which is a substantial economic activity in many places. Fish farming may be an important source of income in rural regions, reducing poverty and raising standards of life.

3. Advantages for the Environment: Compared to other types of animal husbandry, fish farming may have less of an adverse effect on the environment if it is conducted responsibly. Fish, for example, need less feed and emit less greenhouse emissions than land-based animals because they turn grain into protein more effectively. Integrated aquaculture systems may also lessen waste and recycle nutrients, which improves environmental sustainability in general.

4. Enhanced Food Security: By offering a dependable and reasonably priced source of protein, fish farming helps to ensure the availability of food worldwide. Fish is a staple diet in many underdeveloped nations, and aquaculture helps guarantee that this vital resource is accessible all year long. Fish farming helps lower the risk of food shortages and price instability by diversifying the food supply.

5. Better Nutrition: Fish is a great source of vitamins, minerals, and omega-3 fatty acids, among other important nutrients. Fish farming contributes to better nutrition and nutritional variety by expanding the availability of fish via aquaculture, especially in areas where malnutrition is a problem.

Fish Farming System Types

Systems for raising fish differ greatly in terms of size, intricacy, and species they raise. The desired market, the available resources, and the environmental circumstances all influence the system choice. Some of the most popular kinds of fish farming methods are listed below:

1. Pond Systems: One of the most traditional and popular techniques for raising fish is the pond system. Fish are reared in huge, shallow ponds (which may be manmade or natural) under this approach. Pond systems are perfect for small-scale farmers since they are simple to maintain and reasonably priced. They could, however, be vulnerable to problems with water quality and need a lot of land and water supplies.

2. Tank Systems: In-tank systems, fish are raised in large, enclosed tanks composed of plastic, fiberglass, or concrete. More control over the temperature and quality of the water is provided by these systems, which permits more intense agricultural techniques. Recirculating aquaculture systems (RAS), which continually filter and reuse water to reduce water use and environmental effects, often employ tank systems.

3. Cage Systems: In open water environments like lakes, rivers, or coastal regions, cage systems are often used. Fish are kept in huge cages or nets in this arrangement, which is fixed to the water body's bottom. Fish raised in cages may be kept in their natural environment, but they are still susceptible to external events like storms, water pollution, and disease outbreaks.

4. Recirculating Aquaculture Systems (RAS): RAS is a state-of-the-art closed-loop technology for fish farming that recycles water. After being cleaned and filtered to eliminate impurities, the water is cycled back into the

tanks. With the exact control, this technology provides over the rearing environment, fish farming is viable even in regions with limited water supplies or unfavorable climatic circumstances. For high-value species like prawns, trout, and salmon, RAS is often used.

5. Integrated Multi-Trophic Aquaculture (IMTA): This novel method of fish farming includes raising many species in one system while allowing each to contribute to the environment. Seaweed and shellfish, for instance, may be raised alongside fish to help filter the water and provide other cash sources. By minimizing waste and imitating natural ecosystems, IMTA advances sustainability.

6. Aquaponics: This technique combines hydroponics, or growing plants in water, with aquaculture. Fish are kept in tanks in this system, and the waste they produce feeds plants in a linked system

. A symbiotic connection is formed as a result of the plants' assistance in filtering and purifying the water. Aquaponics is a productive and environmentally friendly technique of growing food that enables the production of crops and fish in the same system.

The selection of a fish farming system is contingent upon several aspects, including but not limited to the farmer's objectives, available resources, and the system's location. Each of these systems has pros and cons.

Making wise judgments about starting and running a profitable fish farming business requires an understanding of the many kinds of fish farming systems.

To sum up, fish farming is a vibrant, quickly changing sector that has the potential to significantly contribute to environmental sustainability, economic growth, and global food security. Beginners may make wise judgments and lay the groundwork for a profitable and sustainable fish farming business by learning the fundamentals of the industry, including its significance, history, and different systems.

CHAPTER TWO

Choosing The Correct Type Of Fish

Typical Fish Species For Novices

The correct fish species must be chosen before beginning a fish farming operation to ensure success. It's best for novices to start with species that are resilient, manageable, and appropriate for the area. The following common fish species are excellent for beginners:

1. Tilapia: Because of its versatility and simplicity of growing, tilapia is one of the most popular options for novices. It can be grown in both fresh and brackish water, grows swiftly, and has a great tolerance for changing water conditions. In comparison to other species, tilapia are recognized for having a comparatively low feed conversion ratio, which implies they need less nutrition to grow.

2. Catfish: For inexperienced fish growers, catfish are still another fantastic choice. They are hardy and tolerant of a variety of water conditions, even higher ones. Because catfish are bottom feeders and need less intense maintenance than other species, catfish farming is very simple.

3. Trout: If you reside in an area with a moderate temperature, trout are a fantastic alternative since they thrive in colder water conditions. If you can keep the

water at the right temperature and quality, they are rather simple to farm and are well-known for their superior meat.

4. Bass: If you have access to bigger ponds or lakes, largemouth, and smallmouth bass are popular in North America and may be a wonderful option for novices. Since bass are predatory fish, a healthy ecology with other fish species is necessary for their survival.

5. Carp: Carp have a great degree of adaptability and can live in a variety of aquatic environments. They are especially good for novices in places where the quality of the water varies. Carp farming may need less labor, but in order to prevent overpopulation, it is crucial to carefully control the fish's development and reproduction.

Considerations For Selecting A Species

In order to pick a fish species that will flourish in your setting and help you achieve your farming objectives, it is important to take into account a number of important considerations. Here are a few crucial things to remember:

1. Water Temperature: The ideal temperature for each type of fish varies. It will be easier for you to choose species that can safely survive in the usual water temperature in your location. For example, tilapia and catfish can tolerate warmer conditions better than trout, which prefer colder waters.

2. Water Quality: Fish health is greatly influenced by the pH, dissolved oxygen content, and clarity of the water. Certain species may survive longer in unclean water than others. A more prosperous agricultural enterprise may be achieved by doing routine water testing and selecting species that can adapt to the unique qualities of your water.

3. Space and Habitat: The fish species you choose will depend on the dimensions and design of your aquaculture facility (ponds, tanks, or raceways). While certain species, like catfish and tilapia, can adapt to more regulated settings, others, like bass, need wider areas with natural habitats.

4. Diet and Feeding: The nutritional requirements of different animals vary. It's critical to evaluate the cost and availability of feed for the species you are selecting. It's important to consider feed costs when choosing fish to farm since some fish may be more costly to raise.

5. Market Demand and Economics: It's important to look at the market demand as well as the fish species' economic viability. Selecting species that have a large market demand might result in higher profits. Take into account the expenses related to fish breeding, rearing, and selling.

Fish Species Matching With Climate And Resources

Achieving effective fish farming requires matching the kind of fish you have selected to the resources and environment in your area. Here's how to make sure the species you've chosen fits your resources and environmental conditions:

1. **Climate Adaptability:** When selecting fish species, take your local climate into account. While temperate species like trout are better adapted for colder conditions, tropical species like tilapia do better in warmer climates. Making sure your fish can survive in the environment where they live can lower the chance of illness and increase growth rates overall.

2. **Resource Availability:** Evaluate the facilities, feed, and water sources that are available for your fish farming business. Certain animals can need more specialized resources or better nutrition. For example, tilapia can tolerate a variety of water conditions but may need more feed, but trout farming may require a consistent supply of cool, clean water.

3. **Environmental Impact:** Take into account how the fish species you choose will affect the environment. Certain species have the potential to disrupt local ecosystems if they escape and become more invasive than others. Reducing environmental hazards may be achieved by choosing species that are less prone to upset regional ecosystems.

4. **Economic Feasibility:** Choose a fish species based on your financial situation and objectives. While certain species are more economical to maintain and develop, others can need larger infrastructure investments. Assessing the species' long-term economic effects can

assist you in selecting one that fits both your agricultural goals and your financial situation.

5. Local Regulations: Recognise the rules and laws that apply to fish farming in your area. Regarding fish species, water use, and environmental preservation, different areas have different laws and regulations. Making sure you abide by these rules can help you stay out of trouble with the law.

CHAPTER THREE

Putting Your Fish Farm In Order

Choosing And Setting Up The Site

Selecting an appropriate site is essential to a fish farming business's success. A number of variables that might have a big influence on both the productivity of your farm and the health of your fish are evaluated throughout the site selection process.

1. Source and Quality of Water

The availability and quality of water should be taken into account initially. Fish need clean, oxygenated water to develop and stay healthy. Your location should ideally be close to a dependable water supply, such as a well, river, or spring. Testing should be done on the water supply to determine its hardness, pH, temperature, and pollutant content. It's essential to make sure the water satisfies the requirements of the particular fish species you want to farm since water quality might affect fish growth rates and illness susceptibility.

2. Earth and Soil

Fish pond design and management are significantly influenced by the site's topography and soil composition. In order to hold onto water and stop leaks, the soil should ideally have clayey qualities. Steer clear of locations with rocky or sandy soil as this might allow water to leak out and raise operating expenses. To guarantee that water flows uniformly across the property and to make building ponds easier, the topography should be generally level.

3. Weather and Climate

Fish health and farm management are impacted by climate and weather. Fish may get stressed and have growth-related issues at extreme temperatures, regardless of the temperature. Make sure the local climate is appropriate for the fish species you want to grow by assessing it. For example, cold-water fish demand colder temperatures, but tropical fish prefer warmer settings. Think about seasonal differences and be ready for any weather-related emergencies.

4. Infrastructure and Accessibility

Fish, feed, and equipment should be able to be transported to the location with ease. The effectiveness of agricultural operations may be increased and logistical expenses can be decreased by being close to markets and roadways. Make sure the essential infrastructure is in place or make the appropriate development plans. This involves having access to waste disposal systems, feed and supply storage facilities, and energy for equipment.

5. Impact on the Environment

Assessing the possible environmental effects of your fish farm is crucial. Consider the potential effects of your activities on nearby waterways, animals, and ecosystems. Put into practice strategies to reduce damage to the environment, such as utilizing natural filters, disposing of garbage responsibly, and avoiding the use of hazardous chemicals. Important elements in the site selection process include getting the required permissions and adhering to local environmental standards.

Pond Design And Construction

Building and designing ponds is an important part of starting a fish farm. The design should provide ideal development circumstances and address the unique requirements of the fish species you want to raise.

1. Size and Form of the Pond

The quantity of fish you want to stock and their growing needs should be taken into consideration while designing the pond's size and form. Greater fish populations may be supported by larger ponds, which often provide more stable water conditions. The pond's form might affect the aeration and circulation of the water. Ponds that are round or rectangular are often employed, however the decision may vary depending on the topography and available area.

2. Water Management and Depth

The depth of the pond is essential for preserving the oxygen and temperature of the water. Fish ponds should normally be at least 1.5 to 2 meters deep. Deeper ponds provide a more stable environment and lessen the chance that temperature swings would harm fish. To further maintain ideal conditions and control water levels, think about implementing an input and outflow pipe system for water management.

3. Pond Filtration and Linings

It's crucial to line the pond with an appropriate material to stop water leaks and preserve water quality. Because clay linings naturally have sealing qualities, they are often employed. For enhanced durability, synthetic liners composed of PVC or HDPE may be used as an alternative. A filtration system may be added to assist control waste and maintaining clean water. Filters that are mechanical, biological, or chemical may be employed to get rid of pollutants and waste.

4. Systems of Aeration

Systems for aeration are necessary to guarantee that the water has enough oxygen. Sufficient oxygen concentrations are essential for fish development and well-being. Surface aerators, which stir the water's surface, and diffuser systems, which inject air bubbles into the water, are two types of aeration systems. The size of the pond and the particular oxygen needs of the fish species influence the choice of aeration equipment.

5. Availability and Upkeep

Consider accessibility while designing your pond. Incorporate elements like walkways or platforms that provide simple access to the pond for upkeep, observation, and feeding. To guarantee the lifetime of the pond and the well-being of the fish, regular care is required. Schedule routine maintenance, upkeep, and repairs to take care of any problems as soon as they arise.

Tools & Equipment Needed

Having the appropriate tools and equipment for your fish farm is crucial for effective management and productive fish farming.

1. Kits for Testing Water

To keep your fish in a healthy habitat, regular water quality monitoring is essential. Purchase water testing kits to determine the levels of ammonia, nitrites, nitrates, and pH. These kits assist you in identifying any problems with the quality of the water and implementing any necessary corrections.

2. Feeding apparatus

Your fish's health and development depend on effective feeding. You may need a variety of feeding equipment, such as feeders, dispensers, and storage bins, depending on the size of your business. With the use of automatic feeders, feeding schedules and volumes may be regulated, saving labor and guaranteeing the fish's nutrition.

3. Equipment for Aeration

As was previously noted, aeration is essential to keeping the pond's oxygen levels stable. Provide the right aeration equipment for your farm, such as surface aerators, diffusers, and air pumps. The aeration equipment's size and kind should correspond to the requirements of the fish species in your pond.

4. Harvesting and Netting Equipment

To manage fish populations and carry out routine inspections, netting and harvesting equipment are required. Purchase sturdy seines, nets, and other harvesting tools to handle fish with ease and reduce stress. Make sure the equipment is appropriate for the size and kind of fish you are raising.

5. Tools for Upkeep and Repair

Fish farming involves routine maintenance and repair of infrastructure and equipment. For regular maintenance activities, have a set of basic tools on hand, such as screwdrivers, pliers, and wrenches. Moreover, have repair kits and replacement parts available for last-minute repairs and to save downtime.

6. Tools for Record-keeping and Management

Maintaining thorough records of fish growth, water quality, feeding schedules, and other operational details is necessary for effective management. To monitor and analyze data, use record-keeping tools like spreadsheets or management software. Making well-informed judgments and maximizing farm performance both benefit from this knowledge.

7. Safety Equipment

A major priority in fish farming is safety. Make sure you and your employees are wearing the proper protective clothes, boots, and gloves. Make sure that all safety procedures are followed in order to avoid mishaps and preserve a secure workplace.

CHAPTER FOUR

Management Of Water Quality

Water Quality Is Important

The foundation of an effective fish farming enterprise is water quality. Fish health and growth are immediately impacted, which has an impact on behavior, reproduction, and general well-being. Numerous problems, including disease outbreaks, stunted development, and even mass death, may be brought on by poor water quality. The sustainability of the fish farm and maximum production depend on the understanding and maintenance of appropriate water quality.

The three main elements of water quality are biological, chemical, and physical. Temperature and clarity are two examples of physical variables that affect fish health and feed efficiency. Fish habitat suitability is dependent on chemical elements like pH and dissolved oxygen. The balance of helpful microbes and the existence of pathogens are biological variables.

Sustaining optimal water quality also enhances the agricultural system's overall effectiveness. Fish metabolism is improved, feed conversion rates are increased, and the demand for medical care is decreased in clean, well-oxygenated water. Higher profitability and cost reductions may follow from this.

Essentially, maintaining clean water is just one aspect of water quality management; another is establishing a healthy ecosystem that supports fish growth. Proactive management and regular monitoring are essential to resolving any concerns before they become serious ones.

Keeping An Eye On Water Parameters
pH Scales

pH is a scale from 0 to 14 that indicates how acidic or alkaline the water is. Seven is the neutral pH, seven is the acidic pH, and seven is the alkaline pH. A pH range of 6.5 to 8.5 is preferred by the majority of fish species, however this may change based on the species being raised. A departure from this range may result in stress, slower development, and a higher risk of illness.

Use a trustworthy pH meter or test kit to keep an eye on pH. Testing on a regular basis is essential, particularly after large-scale water treatment or alterations. Adjusters or buffering agents may be used to bring pH levels back into the correct range. For instance, alkaline water's pH may be lowered by acids, whereas acidic water's pH can be raised by adding lime.

The temperature

Temperature has an impact on fish metabolism, which in turn impacts growth, eating habits, and general health. Various species have distinct temperature needs, and it's critical to preserve their ideal ranges. The majority of fish species have a preferred range of temperatures, and going outside of that range may cause stress and lower survival rates.

Digital temperature sensors or thermometers may be used to track temperature. Frequent monitoring of temperature swings is crucial since abrupt shifts in temperature may be dangerous. Heating systems could be required in colder regions while cooling systems or shade might be needed in hot climes. Maintaining a steady temperature within the advised range aids in the preservation of fish health and encourages rapid development.

Levels of Oxygen

Fish breathing and general health depend on dissolved oxygen (DO). Hypoxia, which is brought on by low oxygen levels, may result in stress, stunted development, and even death. The temperature of the water, the rate at which organic matter breaks down, and stocking density all affect oxygen levels.

Use test kits or oxygen meters to keep an eye on dissolved oxygen. Check the oxygen levels often, particularly in high-density tanks or during periods of peak feeding. The use of aeration equipment, such as diffusers and air pumps, may raise the oxygen content. Sustaining proper water circulation and organic waste management may also aid in sustaining sufficient oxygen levels.

Methods For Preserving Water Quality

Systems of Filtration

Filtration systems are necessary to remove impurities, excess nutrients, and particle debris from water. Chemical, biological, and mechanical filters are among the several kinds of filters. While biological filters encourage the development of helpful microorganisms that break down organic waste, mechanical filters remove larger particles. Certain impurities may be eliminated by chemical filters by adsorption or chemical reactions.

To guarantee the efficacy of filtering systems, regular cleaning and maintenance are essential. To prevent clogging and inefficiency, regularly inspect and replace the filter media and keep an eye on the filter's functioning. Clear, pure water is maintained and the likelihood of problems with water quality is decreased when filters are operating properly.

Water Circulation and Exchange

Water exchange is the process of adding new, clean water to part of the system's water supply. This procedure aids in the dilution and elimination of collected pollutants and waste products. Stocking density and feed rates are two examples of the variables that affect the frequency and amount of water exchange.

Water may be reused thanks to recirculating systems, which cleanse and filter the water continually before putting it back in the tank. This technique minimizes water waste and lessens the need for regular water exchange. Recirculation systems must, however, be carefully managed and given routine maintenance in order to function properly.

Control via Biological Means

Utilizing organisms and natural processes, biological control aims to preserve the quality of water. For instance, adding beneficial bacteria may aid in the degradation of organic waste and enhance the quality of the water. Algae and aquatic plants may also aid in oxygenation and the removal of nutrients.

Understanding the balance of microorganisms and avoiding over-reliance on any one technique is essential to managing biological control. In order to make sure that biological control techniques are efficient and do not lead to any imbalances in the system, regular monitoring and modifications are required.

Frequent Inspection and Upkeep The secret to managing water quality effectively is regular monitoring and upkeep. Establish a schedule for evaluating the characteristics of the water and checking the filtration and aeration apparatus on a regular basis. Maintain records of data on water quality so you can monitor changes over time and spot any possible problems. Cleaning and maintaining machinery, modifying water quality parameters as necessary, and quickly resolving issues are all part of proactive maintenance. You can maintain a healthy environment for your fish and stop small concerns from turning into bigger ones by being attentive and responsive.

CHAPTER FIVE

Fish Nutrition And Feeding

Fish Feed Types

A vital element of aquaculture, fish feed affects the general productivity, growth, and health of farmed fish. To ensure the best possible outcomes in fish farming, it is vital to comprehend the many kinds of fish feed that are obtainable.

1. Retail Pellets

The most popular kind of fish feed used in aquaculture is commercial pellets. They are produced in a variety of sizes and compositions to satisfy the dietary requirements of different fish species. Usually, fish meal, plant proteins, vitamins, and minerals are used to make these pellets. They provide a well-rounded diet and are designed to encourage development and improve the health of fish. The pellets are offered in sinking and floating varieties to accommodate the dietary requirements of various fish species.

2. Real-time feed

Fish are fed live feed, which consists of creatures like worms, insects, and tiny crustaceans. Fish that are young or growing are often fed this kind of feed since it offers a natural diet that may promote development and strengthen the fish's immune system. Live feed may be a more involved solution since it has to be supplied by suppliers or maintained as living cultures, but it can be advantageous for certain species.

Another alternative in fish farming is frozen feed, especially for species that have unique nutritional requirements or prefer live food. Typically, entire fish or other marine species that have been frozen to retain their nutritional content are used to make this diet. For supplying vital minerals and ensuring a diverse diet, frozen feed might be a great option. To prevent infection, it has to be handled carefully and frozen before feeding.

4. Size and composition of pellets

The kind of fish and their size determine the size and makeup of the pellets. For example, younger fish need easier-to-eat smaller pellets, but older fish could need larger pellets. Furthermore, the pellets' composition varies; some are designed with a high protein content to promote quick development, while others may be supplemented with vitamins or other minerals to promote general health and resistance to illness.

Feeding Plans And Procedures

To maximize fish development and health in aquaculture, efficient feeding schedules and techniques are essential. Maintaining feeding schedules correctly aids in minimizing waste and obtaining the intended results.

1. How to Calculate Feeding Frequency

The kind of fish and their developmental stage determine how often they are fed. For example, because of their high metabolic rate, young fish or fry usually need many feedings every day. Senior fish, on the other hand, may only be fed once or twice a day. To prevent overfeeding or underfeeding, it's critical to keep an eye on the fish's development and modify the feeding schedule as necessary.

2. Feed Amount

It's important to carefully determine how much feed to give the fish in order to satisfy their nutritional demands without wasting too much. A number of variables, including fish size, water temperature, and feed composition, might influence this. To avoid uneaten feed polluting the water, it is normally advised to give the fish a quantity they can finish in a few minutes.

3. Feeding Methods

The kind of fish and how they eat may influence the feeding methods used. While some fish species like to eat at the bottom and may be better suited for sinking pellets, others are surface feeders and may need floating pellets. Automated feeders may be used to feed fish consistently and on a schedule, saving labor and guaranteeing they get the nourishment they need.

4. Keeping an eye on and modifying feed

To make sure the fish are getting the proper quantity of food, it is crucial to regularly observe them and how they eat. If the fish's development, health, and waste output are observed, it may be determined if the frequency or schedule of feedings has to be changed. This promotes the maintenance of healthy aquatic habitats and maximizes feed efficiency.

The Appropriate Nutrition For Each Stage

For fish to promote growth, health, and reproduction, different nutritional requirements must be met at different phases of their development. Comprehending these prerequisites facilitates the development of suitable feeding tactics.

1. Stage Fry

Fish need a lot of nourishment at the fry stage in order to sustain their fast growth and development. For the development of their immune systems and the construction of bodily tissues, they need a diet high in protein and vital fatty acids. These nutrients are often given to the little fish in a manner that is simple for them to eat by using specially prepared fry feed. This phase is essential for building a solid basis for development and well-being in the future.

2. Young Stage

The dietary needs of fish change when they enter the juvenile stage. To support their ongoing growth and development, they need a balanced diet that includes a variety of proteins, carbs, vitamins, and minerals. Their growing growth and shifting metabolic requirements must be taken into consideration while adjusting the meal. Fish start to acquire their eating habits and preferences at this stage, which might affect the kind of feed that is utilized.

3. Stage of Adulthood

The dietary needs of adult fish vary from those of fry and juvenile fish. The goals of their diet should include controlling body weight, promoting reproductive health, and preserving health. While adult fish may not need as much protein in their diet as young fish do, they still need certain elements to be healthy. These nutrients can be balanced in adult-specialized meals.

4. Stage of Breeding

Particular dietary considerations must be made during the breeding period of captive-bred fish in order to maintain the health of the reproductive system and the development of the eggs. During this time, high-quality diets that include extra nutrients like vitamins and omega-3 fatty acids are often employed. The health of adult fish and their progeny, as well as the success of spawning, depend on proper nutrition throughout the breeding period.

To maintain the best possible health and production, fish must be fed according to specific feeding techniques that are necessary for each stage of their growth. Fish farmers may improve the sustainability of their aquaculture business and get better outcomes by being aware of and attending to these nutritional demands.

CHAPTER SIX

Fish Illness And Illness Control

1. Common Fish Illnesses And Their Signs

Maintaining a healthy fish farm requires understanding common fish infections, which is a crucial component of successful aquaculture. Fish raised for food are often affected by a number of illnesses, and being aware of their signs may aid in prompt diagnosis and treatment.

Parasitic Diseases

In fish aquaculture, parasites are a frequent problem that may seriously harm fish health. On the skin, gills, and fins, external parasites like Ichthyophthirius multifiliis, or Ich, create white cysts. Rapid gill movement, lethargic behavior, and rubbing against things are among the symptoms. Gyrodactylus spp., an additional external parasite, produces excessive mucus production and skin sores that may result in subsequent bacterial infections.

Bacterial Diseases

There are many ways that bacterial infections might appear. Aeromonas species. Loss of appetite, irregular swimming behavior, and ulcerative sores are common side effects of infections. Vibrio spp. Hemorrhagic septicemia, which is marked by crimson streaks on the body and fins, may be brought on by infections and, in extreme instances, can result in fast death. Early detection of these signs is essential for averting epidemics.

fungus-related infections

Even though they are less frequent, fungal infections may happen, especially in stressed fish. Saprolegnia species. is a typical freshwater fungus that forms growths on the skin, gills, and fins that resemble cotton. Fish with fungal infections may show signs of decreased development rates, reduced eating, and lethargy.

infections caused by viruses

Particularly deadly illnesses are those caused by viruses, such as Infectious Haematopoietic Necrosis (IHN) and Koi Herpesvirus (KHV). Koi and ornamental carp that have KHV have significant death rates due to signs such as gill necrosis, lethargy, and irregular swimming. IHN is characterized by hemorrhaging in the exterior body and internal organs, and it affects salmonid species.

2. Proactive Steps And Immunisations

It is significantly more effective to prevent illnesses than to cure them. By taking preventative action, disease breakout risks may be greatly decreased, and a healthy fish population can be maintained.

Stocking and Quarantine Procedures

Using quarantine protocols is essential when adding new fish to a farm. For a minimum of two weeks, newly arrived individuals must be kept apart from the general populace in order to observe any indications of illness. Before being put in the main tank or pond during this time, new fish should be checked for any unusual behavior or symptoms and treated if needed.

Management of Water Quality

It is essential to maintain ideal water quality for fish health. Stress and illness may be avoided by routinely monitoring and controlling water factors including pH, temperature, ammonia levels, and oxygen levels. Maintaining a clean environment and lowering the risk of illness is made easier with proper filtration and regular water changes.

dietary and feeding

Supporting the immune system and maintaining fish health need an adequate diet. Fish's inherent defenses against illness are strengthened by premium fish meals that include the right amounts of vitamins and minerals. Refrain from overfeeding since leftover food may contaminate water and encourage the development of dangerous germs.

Immunization Schedules

Immunizations may guard against some bacterial and viral infections. Disease incidence may be considerably decreased by creating a vaccination regimen based on prevalent illnesses in your area and the species you raise. To find out which vaccinations are right for your fish and when to give them, speak with a veterinary aquaculture expert.

3. Options For Treatment And Procedures For Quarantine

When fish infections do arise, management and containment of the disease are contingent upon appropriate treatment and quarantine protocols. Timely and suitable measures may reduce losses and guarantee the health of your fish.

Options for Treatment

The kind and severity of the illness determine the available treatment choices. Anti-parasitic drugs and salt baths may be useful for parasite infestations. Antibiotics may be given via feed or water to treat bacterial illnesses, but caution must be used in their administration to prevent antibiotic resistance. Antifungal drugs are often used to treat fungal infections.

Procedures for Quarantine

To stop the spread of illness, sick fish must also be quarantined in addition to the initial quarantine for new fish. Isolating sick fish in a different tank and treating them according to their needs are the best practices. This aids in the management of the illness and keeps it from harming the population that is healthy.

Continuous monitoring is required after therapy to make sure the illness has been well controlled. To make sure the fish are recuperating and that their habitat is still favorable to their health, routine health examinations and evaluations of the water's quality should be carried out. Depending on how well the patient is recovering, more therapies or modifications to the management techniques could be necessary.

Maintaining Records and Analysing Them

Improving disease management techniques requires keeping thorough records on fish health, illness incidences, and treatments. Finding trends in these data, assessing the efficacy of therapies, and formulating well-informed plans for future illness care are all aided by their analysis.

A complete strategy that involves identifying symptoms, putting preventative measures in place, and administering the right therapies is necessary for the effective management of fish health and illness. Fish farmers may improve the well-being and efficiency of their aquaculture operations by adhering to these recommendations.

CHAPTER SEVEN

Breeding And The Production Of Fingerlings

1. Methods Of Artificial And Natural Breeding

Fish breeding is essential to fish farming because it produces a consistent supply of fingerlings that can be grown and harvested. To accomplish effective reproduction, both artificial and natural breeding techniques are used; each has pros and problems of its own.

Methods of Natural Breeding

Fish that are allowed to reproduce naturally do so in settings that are similar to their native habitat. This technique may be used to fish farming species that don't need as strict breeding conditions. Usually, the procedure entails:

• Breeding stock selection: Large, healthy, and reproductively mature broodfish are chosen for breeding stock. Given that it impacts both the amount and quality of offspring, proper selection is essential.

• **Setting Up the Environment:** With the right pH, water temperature, and habitat features, the breeding environment should be quite similar to the fish's native habitat. For tilapia and trout, for example, this may include establishing breeding grounds or making sure there are many hiding places.

• **Spawning:** In natural breeding, spawning happens spontaneously when male and female fish are housed together in a regulated setting. To guarantee effective reproduction, keep an eye out for indicators of mating behavior in the fish, such as wooing displays or nest construction.

Methods of Artificial Breeding

Contrarily, artificial breeding is a highly regulated method that makes it possible to precisely alter the breeding environment. It is often used for animals that need certain circumstances or do not reproduce well in captivity. Important actions consist of:

• **Hormone Induction:** To encourage spawning, hormonal therapies are given. Luteinizing Hormone-Releasing Hormone (LHRH) and human Chorionic Gonadotropin (hCG) are examples of common hormones. These hormones aid in the release of sperm in men and ovulation in females.

• **Artificial Insemination:** In a regulated environment, collected eggs and sperm are mixed together. Using this technique, desired features may be enhanced by crossing various strains or species and selecting high-quality gametes.

• Egg Fertilisation and Incubation: During incubation, fertilized eggs are closely supervised. To guarantee excellent survival rates, environmental factors including temperature and oxygen saturation are carefully regulated.

2. Egg Incubation And Hatching

Proper hatching and incubation procedures are essential for the healthy growth of fingerlings once eggs have been fertilized. There are several steps in this procedure, and the surroundings must be closely monitored.

Gathering and Managing Eggs

• Collection: Care must be used while gathering fertilized eggs to prevent harm. In order to reduce stress and physical injury, they are usually removed from breeding tanks or incubators using gentle procedures.

• Cleaning: To get rid of any pollutants or dirt, eggs should be cleansed. This aids in avoiding fungal infections and other problems that can hinder the success of hatching.

Conditions of Incubation

• Temperature: It's critical to maintain the proper temperature. There are several temperature ranges for different fish species that are best for egg development.

For example, trout eggs often need colder temperatures than tilapia eggs.

• **Water quality: Care must be taken to monitor ammonia concentrations, pH, and oxygen levels. Water that is pure and well-oxygenated is essential for the proper growth and hatching of eggs.**

• **Monitoring and Adjustments: Ensuring that conditions stay stable requires regular inspections of the incubation environment. If there are any variations, including those in the water's quality or temperature, adjustments can be required.**

Emergence

• **Hatching Process: Depending on the species, eggs usually hatch within a certain amount of time. Keep an eye out for clues that indicate hatching, such as greater egg movement or the development of small embryos.**

• **Post-Hatching Care: After hatching, the larvae or fry should be moved to a rearing tank that has the right environment for their early growth. For them to survive and flourish at this period, proper management is essential.**

3. Handling Of Juveniles And Fingerlings

For fingerlings and juveniles to grow and develop healthily, proper care is necessary. In order to guarantee that they attain maturity, this stage entails regulating their surroundings, food, and overall health.

Nutrition and Feeding

• food Formulation: Fingerling development depends on the provision of balanced food. Premium feeds are designed to satisfy the dietary requirements of fish during various developmental phases. Minerals, vitamins, lipids, and proteins are examples of ingredients.

• Feeding Frequency: Compared to adults, fingerlings often need to be fed frequently. Throughout the day, a few modest feedings serve to guarantee appropriate development and lower the possibility of overfeeding or underfeeding.

• Monitoring Growth: Frequent evaluations of eating patterns and growth rates assist in identifying if dietary modifications are required. Vibrant, healthy fingerlings should exhibit steady growth and positive feeding reactions.

Management of the Environment

• Tank Conditions: Keep raising tanks' water quality at its best. It is crucial to regularly check variables like temperature, pH, and oxygen levels in order to avoid stress and illness.

• Space and Density: Give the fish enough room to develop so as to prevent overpopulation. Appropriate stocking densities lower the chance of disease outbreaks and stop competition for resources.

Medical Administration

• **Disease Prevention: Take proactive steps to avoid illness, such as being vaccinated, getting regular checkups, and keeping your surroundings clean. Treat any anomalies or indications of sickness right away to avoid more serious problems.**

• **Record-keeping: Keep thorough records of your child's development, feeding patterns, and medical observations. Making educated judgments regarding the care of the fish and managing the farm both benefit from this knowledge.**

CHAPTER EIGHT

Gathering And Preparing

When To Harvest And How To Harvest

Recognizing the Best Harvesting Times

For your fish farming business to be profitable and of high quality, timing is everything when it comes to fish harvesting. The kind of fish, how quickly they develop, and the needs of the market all influence the best time to harvest. Harvesting is usually completed for many fish species when the fish reaches a size or weight that satisfies market requirements. To find the ideal time to harvest, it is crucial to constantly assess fish development using growth charts and measuring instruments.

Considering the Seasons

The time of fish harvesting may be greatly impacted by seasonal variations. The ideal time to harvest fish in temperate areas might be affected by fish development rates that slow down in the winter. Conversely, fish may thrive more reliably all year round in warmer areas or regulated settings like aquaponics systems. By being aware of the seasonal variations in your species of fish, you can ensure high-quality fish and increase productivity by modifying your harvesting schedule appropriately.

Methods of Harvesting

Fish may be harvested using a variety of techniques, each having pros and downsides of its own. The most popular techniques consist of:

• Netting: In this technique, fish are removed from their natural habitat by use of nets. You may use a variety of nets, such as dip nets for smaller tanks or seine nets for bigger regions, depending on the size of your fish farm. Because of its effectiveness and little disruption to the fish, netting is often preferred.

• Trapping: A more regulated method of capturing fish is achieved via the use of traps. They may be arranged to draw fish into a small area so that they can be conveniently gathered. For smaller-scale operations or certain fish species that react well to traps, this technique is very helpful.

• Culling: Culling is the process of eliminating fish from a stock in a selected manner according to factors like size, condition, or other factors. This technique reduces competition and overpopulation, which helps the surviving fish develop and thrive more generally.

After-Harvest Management

Fish should be treated carefully after harvesting to avoid damage and guarantee excellent quality. Minimizing stress on the fish, preventing lengthy exposure to air, and using clean, sanitized equipment are all examples of proper handling procedures. Fish must be moved quickly to a processing center or storage facility in order to keep it fresh and avoid spoiling.

Methods For Processing Fish

First Processing Stages

To guarantee that the fish are ready for sale or further processing, there are a few crucial procedures involved in the first processing of the fish. These actions consist of:

• Cleaning: The scales, intestines, and internal organs of the fish are removed during the cleaning procedure. Typically, specialized tools or equipment are used for this in order to assure completeness and reduce contamination. Cleaning may also include filleting the fish or removing the bones from species like fish that have edible bones.

• Filleting: The technique of slicing fish into fillets, or boneless sections of the fish, is known as filleting. To guarantee that the fillets are of the highest quality and devoid of bones, this procedure requires accuracy and expertise. Depending on the size of your business, filleting may be done manually or with the aid of automated equipment.

• Skinning: To enhance the texture and look of the fillets, the skin of certain fish species is removed. Depending on the size and kind of fish, skinning may be done using a knife or a skinning machine.

Advanced Methods of Processing

For goods with added value, the following further processing methods might be used:

• Smoking: Fish that has been smoked improves flavor and keeps longer. The fish is cured with salt or other preservatives before being exposed to smoke from burning wood or other materials in the smoking process. There are several ways to smoke, including as hot and cold smoking, and each results in a unique flavor and texture.

• Freezing: Fish may be effectively preserved and have its shelf life extended by freezing it. Fish may be frozen whole or in fillets, but to avoid freezer burn and preserve quality, freezing procedures must be followed. The texture and flavor of the fish are best preserved by using rapid freezing techniques like blast freezing.

• Canning: Canning is an additional fish preservation technique, particularly for long-term storage. The fish is cooked in enclosed containers and then subjected to heat processing to eliminate any germs or other pathogens. Fish items in cans are popular in a variety of markets because they are handy and have a long shelf life.

Fish Harvested: Preservation And Storage

Quick Storage

Fish has to be kept carefully after processing in order to preserve its freshness and quality. Considerations for immediate storage consist of:

• Temperature Control: Fish should be kept at the proper temperature to avoid spoiling. Fish should be kept refrigerated at or below 4°C (39°F) in order to prevent bacterial development and preserve freshness. Freezing is advised for extended storage to avoid spoiling.

• Sanitation: In order to avoid contamination, storage facilities must be kept clean and sanitized. This includes routinely cleaning refrigerated units, storage tanks, and other fish handling and storage equipment.

Putting together

When storing and transporting fish, proper packaging is essential to maintaining fish quality. Typical packing techniques include:

• Vacuum sealing: By eliminating air from packing, vacuum sealing prolongs shelf life and helps avoid freezer burn. This approach works well for both whole fish and fillets, and it works especially well with frozen fish.

• Cryovac Packaging: This technique involves vacuum-sealing fish in plastic pouches and then heat-sealing the container. This technique helps keep freshness and avoid contamination and is often used for retail packaging.

• Ice Packing: Fish packed in ice may assist in maintaining the right temperature and prevent spoiling during short-term storage or transit. Fresh fish that will be sold directly to customers or distributors is often packaged in ice.

Observation and Control of Quality

To guarantee quality and stop spoiling, seafood that has been preserved has to be continuously observed. Frequent checks of the package integrity, temperature controls, and general storage conditions may assist spot such problems before they have an impact on the fish. You can make sure that your fish products live up to industry standards and consumer expectations by putting quality control procedures into place and keeping thorough records of handling procedures and storage conditions.

CHAPTER NINE

Promoting And Getting Rid Of Your Fish

Finding The Right Target Markets

Knowing your target market is essential to developing methods that work when it comes to marketing and selling fish. This entails figuring out who is most likely to purchase your seafood and adjusting your strategy to suit their requirements.

1. Recognising Local Demographics: Start by doing a local area analysis. Who may be your target clientele? Are they local grocery businesses, eateries, or families? For instance, if your business is located close to a seaside town, a sizable section of your market can be seafood enthusiasts. You may better match your offers with consumer demand by having an understanding of local consumption trends and preferences.

2. Investigating Niche Markets: Take into account focussing on underserved niche markets in your community. This might include upscale eateries searching for specialty or gourmet fish, health-conscious customers looking for fresh or organic products, or even neighborhood pet businesses in need of fish for aquariums. To learn about certain requirements and preferences, investigate and interact with these niches.

3. Leveraging Market Research: To acquire information about your possible clientele, make use of market research instruments and methodologies. Industry studies, focus groups, and surveys may all provide insightful information on the purchasing habits, preferences, and behavior of customers. With the use of this data, you may more successfully address consumer requests by customizing your product offers and marketing initiatives.

4. Creating Customer Profiles: From your study, create thorough customer profiles. Make personas that reflect the various groups of your target market, taking into account their issues, preferences, and purchasing habits. This aids in targeting the particular requirements of every consumer niche and personalizing your marketing campaigns.

5. Developing Relationships: Reaching out to neighborhood companies and civic associations might lead to new business opportunities. For example, entering into supply arrangements with nearby restaurants or grocery shops helps guarantee consistent demand. To make connections with possible partners and customers, go to trade exhibits, networking events, and neighborhood gatherings.

Strategies For Pricing And Profit Margin

Maintaining a competitive edge in the market, meeting profit margin requirements, and paying expenditures all need careful consideration when setting your fish's price. Here's how to create winning price plans:

1. To calculate expenses, first make sure you are aware of every expense related to fish farming. Feed, tools, labor, utilities, and upkeep are all included in this. Making accurate cost calculations guarantees that the prices you set will cover costs and increase your profit margin.

2. Examining Market Prices: Find out how your local rivals are charging for comparable goods. It's helpful to know the average market price for various fish varieties so you can set competitive rates. Make sure the cost of your product accurately corresponds to its value and distinctiveness.

3. Establishing Profit Margins: Using your cost estimates and market research, ascertain the profit margins you would want to have. Strive for a profit margin that allows for adequate profitability and pays expenses. To attract diverse consumer groups and maximize income, think about establishing tiered pricing for different fish varieties or amounts.

4. Providing Value-Added Goods: To support higher pricing, think about adding value to your fish goods. This can include providing extra services like delivery or pre-packaged or prepared seafood. Products with additional value may help set your business apart from the competition and fetch greater pricing.

5. Changing with the Market: Be ready to modify your price plans in response to consumer input and market developments. Make sure your prices are competitive and accurately represent any adjustments to your cost structure or changes in the market by reviewing them on a regular basis. Maintaining market share and consumer interest is facilitated by price flexibility.

Channels Of Distribution And Sales Advice

To get your fish to market and increase sales, you need to use efficient distribution routes and sales strategies. Here's how to maximize each of these factors:

1. Choosing Distribution Channels: Make sure the channels you choose support both your company plan and your target market. This might include wholesale distribution to eateries and supermarkets, or direct sales to customers via farmers' markets or internet platforms. Select the channels that best suit your company's demands since each has unique logistical and financial concerns.

2. Creating a Sales plan: Create a sales plan that emphasizes your fish's special selling features. Make sure to express these advantages to prospective customers, whether they are related to sustainability, freshness, or unusual species. Create promotional materials to highlight your fish and draw in clients, such as websites, pamphlets, and social media posts.

3. Creating Partnerships: You may expand your market reach by establishing solid connections with retailers, distributors, and other partners. In order to guarantee seamless distribution procedures, agree on advantageous conditions and keep lines of contact open. Work together with partners on marketing initiatives to increase sales and exposure.

4. Ensuring Quality Control: Throughout the distribution process, uphold strict quality control requirements. To maintain the freshness and quality of your fish, make sure it is handled correctly. Strict quality control and adherence to food safety laws foster consumer confidence and lower the possibility of returns or complaints.

5. Making the Most of Sales Channels: Make the most of your sales channels by using data and technology. Track sales, handle orders, and examine client behavior using customer relationship management (CRM) systems. This data enhances client service and helps you hone your sales tactics.

CHAPTER TEN

Budgeting And Financial Planning

Setup Fees At First And Continued Charges

It's important to have a thorough grasp of both the setup and running costs before beginning a fish farming business. The viability and sustainability of your fish farm will be determined by the completion of this financial foundation.

Initial Expenses of Setup

The fees you'll spend before your fish farm is operational are included in the initial setup charges. These consist of leasing or buying land, which will take up a significant amount of your initial funding. Costs of land may vary significantly depending on size and location. It is necessary to take into account land preparation, which includes terrain modification to meet your agricultural demands as well as cleaning and leveling the ground.

Another large expense is infrastructure construction. Building ponds or tanks, putting in water supply systems, and putting in filtration and aeration systems are all included in this. To keep your fish in a healthy habitat, each of these elements is necessary. The species you choose and the size of your business will determine the kind and amount of infrastructure.

Supplies and equipment also go towards your initial costs. This involves buying feed, water testing kits, fish fry or fingerlings, and other essential materials. You'll also need to spend money on transportation so that your supplies and fish can be delivered.

Continuous Outlays

After your fish farm is operational, you will have continuous costs that are essential to day-to-day operations. Usually, the biggest recurrent expenditure is feed. The kind and amount of feed required will vary depending on the species and development stage of the fish. To guarantee ideal circumstances for fish development and well-being, routine water quality monitoring and treatment are also required.

Labor expenses are yet another continuous expenditure. Depending on the scale of your business, you may need to recruit workers for a variety of jobs including equipment management, cleaning, feeding, and health monitoring for the fish. Utilities, such as water and electricity, will also have an effect on your budget. It's also essential to do routine maintenance on infrastructure and equipment to avoid expensive repairs and guarantee efficient functioning.

Strategies for Financial Planning

Creating a thorough financial strategy is essential to controlling these costs. Make a budget that accounts for both setup fees upfront and recurring charges. You'll be able to keep an eye on your expenses and make wise choices using this. Reviewing and modifying your budget on a regular basis can help you remain on target and deal with any unforeseen financial difficulties.

Assessing the financial feasibility of your fish farming endeavor requires an understanding of its profitability and return on investment (ROI). ROI gives you information about the long-term viability of your business and assists you in determining how well your investment is producing profits.

How To Determine Profitability

You may assess profitability by contrasting your income and costs. Compute the market price of your fish and project the projected yield depending on your capacity for production to get an idea of possible income. Take into account variables like fish growth and survival rates as well as market demand. To get your net profit, deduct your ongoing costs (feed, labor, utilities, and maintenance) from your income.

Assessing Return on Investment

Profitability in relation to investment cost is measured by return on investment, or ROI. Utilize the following formula to determine ROI:

ROI=(Total InvestmentNet Profit)×100\text{ROI} = \left(\frac{\text{Total Investment}}{\text{Net Profit}} \right) \times 100ROI=(Total InvestmentNet Profit)×100

67

Where Total Investment includes both the original setup expenditures and any extra investments made during the operation, and Net Profit is the revenue less the expenses. An enterprise that has a greater ROI is more lucrative.

Amounts Influencing ROI

ROI may be impacted by a number of variables, such as fish prices, production efficiency, and market circumstances. The selling price of your fish may be impacted by changes in the market, and the cost of labor and feed is influenced by the efficiency of production. ROI may be increased by keeping a regular eye on these variables and making necessary adjustments to your operations.

Increasing Earnings

Thinking about streamlining your manufacturing processes might help increase profitability. This might include raising fish growth rates, reducing waste, and optimizing feed conversion rates. Look at methods to save expenses, such as obtaining more affordable equipment or negotiating better feed prices. Additionally, you may increase overall profitability and generate new income streams by expanding your product line or investigating value-added items.

Financial Management And Funding Alternatives

Getting enough money and handling money well is essential to your fish farming business's success.

Investigate different financing sources and put good financial management techniques into place to make sure your business can survive.

Finances Available

Fish farming endeavors might choose from a variety of financing sources. For many beginning farmers, personal savings serve as their main source of finance. This may not always be enough to pay for everything, however. Take into account applying for loans from banks or government initiatives meant to assist with farming endeavors. These loans could come with cheaper interest rates and better conditions.

Financial assistance may also come from grants and subsidies given by government departments or nonprofit organizations. Examine the local programs that are offered, then submit grant applications that support your objectives for fish farming. In addition, should you want to expand your business considerably, you may look into venture capital or investment alternatives.

Money Handling

Keeping track of your earnings and outlays, controlling cash flow, and making sure loan and bill payments are made on time are all necessary for good financial management. To keep proper financial records, use accounting software or engage an accountant. To keep an eye on your cash flow and profitability, go over your financial accounts on a regular basis.

You may better control expenditures and increase profitability by putting cost-management measures into place. To lower utility expenses, haggle with suppliers for cheaper feed and equipment pricing. You may also look into energy-efficient choices. Create a financial backup plan as well in case of unforeseen costs or changes in income.

Extended-Term Budgeting

To keep your fish farming business viable, long-term financial planning is necessary. Create a financial strategy that details your objectives, spending limits, and expansion tactics. Review and revise your strategy often to accommodate shifting market dynamics and operational requirements. Create an emergency fund to handle unanticipated costs and guarantee the operation's stability.

CHAPTER ELEVEN

Ecological Fish Farming Methods

Effects On The Environment And Conservation

Overview of Environmental Impact

Aquaculture, or fish farming, has great promise for producing a large amount of the seafood consumed worldwide. Its development, nevertheless, has to be carefully controlled to reduce negative effects on the environment. In order to prevent fish farming from having a detrimental impact on aquatic ecosystems or adding to ecological imbalances, sustainable techniques are crucial.

Effects on Regional Ecosystems

The influence that fish farming has on regional ecosystems is one of the main issues. The establishment of farms has the potential to damage biodiversity and local environments. When non-native species are introduced, they may compete with native species, changing the ecological balance of the area. Furthermore, the use of pesticides and antibiotics might degrade the quality of the nearby water, endangering the local plant and animal life.

Management of Effluent

Improper management of fish farm effluent, which comprises chemicals, uneaten feed, and fish waste, may have negative impacts on the quality of water. When water bodies become excessively loaded with nutrients, a condition known as eutrophication occurs. This causes excessive algae growth, which lowers oxygen levels and endangers aquatic life. Excess nutrients from effluent may cause this.

Strategies for Mitigation

There are many techniques that fish farms might use to lessen these effects. Recirculating aquaculture systems (RAS) are one method that reduces pollution output by filtering and reusing water. Additionally, by cultivating supplementary species that make use of the waste products from the principal fish, integrated multi-trophic aquaculture (IMTA) systems may aid in the recycling of nutrients.

Preservation Activities

Conserving wild fish populations and their habitats is another goal of sustainable fish farming operations. Farms should support conservation efforts that save natural ecosystems and refrain from obtaining fish feed from overfished fisheries. Guidelines and criteria are provided by certification programs, including those offered by the Aquaculture Stewardship Council (ASC) and the Marine Stewardship Council (MSC), to guarantee ecologically acceptable activities.

Participation in the Community

Involving stakeholders and local communities is essential to the success of sustainable fish farming. In order to solve issues and incorporate traditional ecological knowledge into their operations, farms should collaborate with local organizations. This strategy can guarantee that fish farming maintains rather than damages regional ecosystems by striking a balance between economic gains and environmental care.

Recycling And Waste Management

Overview of Waste Management

To reduce fish farms' environmental impact, waste management must be done well. In addition to lowering pollution, proper waste management improves the sustainability of fish farming operations. To end the resource use loop, waste management techniques should prioritize reducing, reusing, and recycling.

categories of waste produced

trash comes from fish farms in several forms: solid trash (dead fish and debris), chemical waste (medications and disinfectants), and organic waste (fish feces and uneaten feed). To reduce its negative effects on the environment, different waste types need different treatment techniques.

Management of Organic Waste

There are many ways to handle organic waste, including fish poop and uneaten feed. Using biofilters, which employ microorganisms to break down organic materials, is one efficient technique. A further strategy is to use aquaponics systems, which create a closed-loop system that is advantageous to both fish and plants by using fish waste as plant fertilizer.

Management of Chemical Waste

To avoid contaminating water sources, chemical waste, including antibiotics and other treatments, has to be managed carefully. In order to properly store and dispose of chemicals, farms should adhere to the best standards, which include secure containment and appropriate labeling. The use of natural medicines and probiotics as substitute therapies may help lessen the need for pharmacological interventions.

Resource Recovery and Recycling

The recovery of resources and recycling are essential elements of sustainable waste management. Waste from fish farms may be processed to produce profitable byproducts like fish meal, which is used as animal feed. Composting dead fish and other organic materials or using them to produce biogas are two ways to produce sustainable energy.

Putting Best Practices Into Practice

Fish farms should create and adhere to a thorough waste management strategy in order to perform efficient recycling and waste management procedures.

Regular waste stream monitoring and evaluation, staff training on proper waste management techniques, and technology purchases that facilitate resource recovery and waste reduction should all be part of this strategy.

Strategies For Long-Term Sustainability

Overview of Long-Term Sustainability

Fish farming must use measures that maintain industrial profitability while safeguarding the environment and assisting local people if it is to be long-term sustainable. To be successful over the long run, sustainable fish farming methods need to take social, environmental, and economic factors into account.

Financial Sustainability

For fish farming businesses to be successful over the long term, economic sustainability is crucial. Farms need to concentrate on raising output and efficiency levels, controlling expenses, and optimizing profits. Incorporating value-added goods or eco-tourism, for example, might help diversify revenue sources and improve economic stability.

Protection of the Environment

Environmental protection is essential to long-term viability. Fish farms should use eco-friendly techniques including protecting biodiversity, cutting down on pollution, and using less water. Ecosystem health may be preserved by putting best practices for environmental management and habitat restoration into practice.

Social Accountability

In order to achieve social sustainability, local communities' and workers' demands and concerns must be addressed. Fair compensation, secure working conditions, and chances for skill advancement should all be offered by fish farms. Getting involved in local communities and lending assistance to social projects may foster goodwill and improve the area's overall well-being.

Investigation and Originality

Investing in innovation and research is essential to the advancement of sustainable fish farming methods. Farms should keep up with the most recent scientific and technological advancements in order to enhance procedures and handle new problems. Working together with academic institutions and business leaders may spur innovation and advance environmentally friendly solutions.

Observation and Assessment

In order to determine if sustainability initiatives are successful, ongoing monitoring and assessment are necessary. Fish farms should monitor their success, establish quantifiable targets, and assess their procedures on a regular basis. Third-party audits and certification programs may guarantee sustainability requirements are followed and provide insightful comments.

Conclusion

Considering the Trip

Fish farming may be an exciting and intimidating endeavor to begin with. It is important to consider the important turning points in your journey and the vast amount of information you have gained as you near the finish of this course. The goal of this conclusion is to summarise the major ideas discussed in the book and provide a road map for advancing confidently in your fish farming pursuits.

Important Ideas

Understanding the fundamentals—such as choosing the correct species, creating the ideal habitat, and preserving ideal water quality—is the cornerstone of a successful fish farming enterprise. We've looked at a variety of fish species that are good for novices, such as catfish and tilapia, each with its own needs and advantages. We also spoke about the complexities of planning and maintaining ponds or fish tanks, emphasizing important elements like temperature regulation, aeration, and filtration.

It has been noted that maintaining water quality is essential to a successful fish farm. To avoid illness and preserve fish health, it is essential to regularly check and manage factors including pH, ammonia, nitrites, and nitrates. We also spoke about feeding techniques and the value of a well-balanced diet in fostering your fish's development and lifespan.

Proceeding Forward

Now that you have the information and abilities from this book, you are ready to begin your fish farming endeavors. But it's essential that you approach this endeavor with an attitude of constant learning and flexibility. Aquaculture is a dynamic area where best practices and innovations change over time. Keeping up with the latest advancements and modifying your strategies appropriately can help ensure your success in the long run.

Looking for More Sources

If you want to improve your experience with fish farming, you should look for more resources, such as publications from the industry, internet forums, and local aquaculture groups. Making connections with seasoned fish farmers and going to conferences or seminars might provide insightful information and useful guidance. In addition, in case you run into difficulties or want specific advice, don't be afraid to seek advice from specialists or professionals in the industry.

Last Words

In conclusion, for those who are prepared to put in the time and effort to learn about the intricacies of aquaculture, fish farming is a lucrative opportunity. You may start a profitable and long-lasting fish farming business by using the methods and strategies described in this article. Recall that attaining your objectives and maintaining the health and productivity of your fish depends on perseverance, commitment, and ongoing learning.